Lost Lake

Other Ziggurat Books by
Marcus Reichert

Confessions: Poems by Marcus Reichert
Hoboken: A Novel
Art & Ego: Marcus Reichert
in Conversation with Edward Rozzo
Displaced Person:
Poetry, Pornography and Politics
(Selected Writings 1970-2005)

Lost Lake

Early Poems
by
Marcus Reichert

*Introduction
by
Antony Copley*

ZIGGURAT BOOKS
International

Lost Lake: Early Poems
Copyright © 2012 by Marcus Reichert
Juvenilia: An Introduction
Copyright © 2012 by Antony Copley

All rights reserved. Except for brief passages quoted in a newspaper, magazine, radio, or television program, no part of this book may be reproduced in any form or by any means, electronic or mechanical, including photocopying and recording, or by any information storage and retrieval system, without permission in writing from the Publisher.

Front cover photograph:
Marcus Reichert 1967 (detail) by Edward Rozzo

UK office: 27 St. Quentin House, Fitzhugh Grove,
London SW18 3SE, England
Editorial office: 6 rue Argenterie,
30170 St. Hippolyte du Fort, France
Enquiries: zigguratbooks@orange.fr

Printed in England by Imprint Academic
Seychelles Farm, Upton Pyne, Exeter, Devon EX5 5HY

Distributed by Central Books Ltd.
99 Wallis Road, London E9 5LN, England
Tel UK: 0845 458 9911
Fax UK: 0845 459 9912
Tel International: +44 20 8525 8800
Fax International: +44 20 8525 8879
E-mail: orders@centralbooks.com

First Edition

ISBN 978-0-9566579-7-8

Marcus Reichert is a painter and a poet who has also worked in film. His film works are held in the Archive of the Museum of Modern Art, New York. His Crucifixion paintings have been described by Richard Harries, the Bishop of Oxford, as being among the most disturbing painted in the 20th Century. Marcus Reichert lives and works in the south of France.

Antony Copley is an Honorary Reader and Honorary Senior Research Fellow in the School of History, University of Kent. He is Academic Adviser to the Gandhi Foundation (UK), and a Fellow of the Royal Historical Society and a Fellow of the Royal Asiatic Society. He is a regular reviewer for the Journal of the Royal Asiatic Society and has published books on sexual morality in France, evangelical missionaries in India, and the Indian politicians, Gandhi and Rajagopalachari. His *A Spiritual Bloomsbury: Hinduism and Homosexuality in the Lives and Writings of Edward Carpenter, E.M. Forster and Christopher Isherwood* (Lexington, 2006) has been republished in India by Yoda Press under the title *Gay Writers in Search of the Divine*.

Marcus Reichert, Saint Hippolyte du Fort, 2011 (Mark Luscombe-Whyte)

Contents

Juvenilia by Antony Copley ix

I.
Lost Lake 1

II.
In the Land of Dirt Farms 13

III.
Poems Written on Glass 19

IV.
Diary of the Plague 37

V.
Darkness: Selected Poems

Blood Flower 45

Day of Africa 46

Destroying the Vestiges 47

The Shaman Leaps 48

The Sabine Women 49

The Angel Morpheus 50

Young Pagan Journeying 52

Hymn of the Scared Heart 53

Man Swimming 54

As Mortals Build Edifices 55

Roses of Remanence 56

Rimbaud Knelt Helplessly 57

Juvenilia
by Antony Copley

It takes some courage to publish one's juvenilia. And this is unusually precocious verse written between the ages of 14 and 19, between 1962 and 1967. The poetry of adolescence always runs the risk self-centredness and pretentiousness. We have at the time such a morbid sense of our own self-importance. But there is a paradox. It is also the time when we express ourselves with the greatest immediacy, with a rawness and a lyricism. Surely the best poetry of the Romantics and of the generation of poets of the 1930s was their earliest. So for Marcus Reichert this is a risk worth running. Admittedly, he destroyed much of this juvenilia at the age of 24 but by luck some had survived in his bedroom at home and rather fortuitously turned up later in New York.

Reichert has provided some clues as to where this poetry comes from in a literary sense. A late reader – reading just sort of happened at the age of 9 or 10 – he was to be highly precocious, devouring James Joyce's *Ulysses* at the age of 12, along with Balzac, Walt Whitman, then too the French writers, Camus, Baudelaire, Nerval, Isadore Ducasse, Rimbaud, but only at the age of 18, Artaud. He was fascinated by the relationship between Eliot and Pound. And then there was Shakespeare. Such precocious reading does much to explain the extremely sophisticated language of the juvenilia, if also the occasional need to turn to the dictionary.

This is free verse. Personally, I have a great respect for the more disciplined verse of rhyme and metre. I have been reading the highly formalised verse of fellow South Asianist and expert on Rabindranath Tagore, William Radice. But if Reichert lacks the discipline of such formalism he compensates with the exceptional intelligence of the language. Quite where this comes from remains a teasing question, though one influence is surely the symbolist poetry of Baudelaire and Rimbaud.

What is the content of the juvenilia? Its strongest element is landscape. Reichert was responding to the landscape of the coal regions of Pennsylvania, with their slag heaps and abandoned mining structures. It conjures up parallels with JG Ballard's dystopian post-industrial landscapes, Steinbeck's barren midwest, the desolation of Wim Wenders' *Paris, Texas*. But he discovered a magic retreat, his own version of Alain Fournier's *Le Grands Meaulnes*. By then the family had moved to Detweiler farm in Collegeville, on the road to Philadelphia. In walking distance from the farm were Hunsberger's Woods and deep within the woods he discovered a small reservoir, a rubbish tip nearby. This is the inspiration for the poetry of *Lost Lake*. Here were the beginnings of his relationship with primordial nature. As he describes it in *Art & Ego*(1), `there were extraordinary things to look at, like the murky reservoir shrouded by tall trees, its dark corners patterned in floating leaves, its mesmerising surface occasionally disrupted by the shimmering of a snake.'(p24) Compare this from a prose poem in the juvenilia: `I often saw myself drowning in a lost lake of venomous pit vipers and submerged derelict cars, infinity eclipsing itself in their surfaces.'(*Lost Lake* p14)

But the lost lake did not provide sufficient withdrawal from the pressure of home so with extraordinary recklessness he set out into a shark infested sea and had to be rescued by the lifeguards. It is not as if home was that uncomprehending, for his father was a fellow artist, but the young poet felt all the imprisonment of the misunderstood and a desperate need to escape. In the end he did so by going in 1965 to Paris: `I had been carried away from pond and farm to watchful towers in the sky.'(*Lost Lake* p37) And then he began visiting his brother in New York City which led to an even greater sense of alienation, if you like, subject to that terrible Sartrean pressure of material objects. It brings to mind a line from early Spender: `the city climbs in horror to my brain.' But Paris was the exception. Here he no longer felt an outcast and at last was at one with the civilised world.

In the final section of the juvenilia, Darkness, we encounter a far bleaker mood. At the age of 11 or 12 Reichert identified with Christ: `I had the overwhelming feeling that I too would be sacrificed, but I would be sacrificed for the simple fact of being alive.' His life would be meaningless, `especially meaningless because I simply couldn't believe there was a God who would grant me eternal life.'(*Art & Ego* p70) In fact there is only one reference to Christ in the juvenilia.(*Lost Lake* p53) The psychologists will have something to say about this adolescent quest for martyrdom. Maybe it is not so unusual. At the age of 17, stuck in a tent in an army camp, part of our CCF training, I felt a calling to lay down my life in the struggle in South Africa against apartheid. No doubt in my reading T.S. Eliot at the time, with his obsession with martyrdom in *Murder in the Cathedral* and Celia's martyrdom in Africa, crucified upside down on an anthill in *The Cocktail Party*, lies an explanation.

If this was not a sufficient burden to bear, Reichert, with an exceptionally strong burgeoning libido, had to bear the sorrow of the girl($_2$) he then loved being diagnosed with Hodgkins's disease at the age of 14 or 15, to die of it at the age of 19. Just possibly some sensibilities might here have been spared and a certain obscurantism might have been applied to an expression of the dictates of this sexuality.

I have a hunch that all of Reichert's later aesthetics stem from the experience of writing the juvenilia. Even at this stage he was furiously battling with the need to be true to one's initial instinctive response and against the later artifice of representation. This is the Judas principle, `the deceit of retrospective bargaining,' the betrayal of our visions when they are no longer immediate; we have surrendered the role of 'shaman, artists of magic.' How can we, free of the corruption of reflection, find our way back to 'the euphoric fountainhead'? (In the Land of Dirt Farms: First Half of Childhood, *Lost Lake* p13) Reichert's was never to be Wordworth's recollection in tranquillity: 'I find renegotiating the past almost impossible.'(*Art & Ego* p10) Premeditated art leaves him cold. Reichert seeks an intuitive expression: this is the way to communicate subliminally with the viewer. 'It's about finding the inexplicable meaning in what we see.' Here Reichert defines what be believes poetry to be: 'depending upon the visceral extremity of the subject, that poetry may be horrific and excruciating to experience but it is nevertheless the manifestation of a sensibility – the artist's sensibility – in pursuit of meaning, no matter how abstract or elusive that meaning might be.'(*Art & Ego* p103) This reaches out to the spiritual and the mystical. Reichert is seeking to move outside conventional time and space: 'Is stair-step time so easily vaulted?'(*Lost Lake* p47) A reference to the atman (*Lost Lake* p65) hints at some awareness of Hindu Vedantism.

There are obvious risks in poetry of this character. He sees virtue in the very elusiveness of the meaning of the poetry: 'I believe if there is a meaning in any work of art it is necessarily elusive.'(*Art and Ego* p37) Indeed, so much of modern poetry seemingly relies for its effect on its being on the border of what we can understand. It runs the risk of mere obscurantism. And it runs a graver risk, though one Reichert recognises, of running into a narcissistic cul-de-sac. In so much of modern art, 'Our identity has been our *ultimate* work of art.'(*Art and Ego* p98)

One curious omission in the juvenilia is any reference to politics. In Paris was he unaware of the recent ferocious struggle over Algeria? I vividly recall in my time in Paris, admittedly a few years earlier, 1961-2, being caught up in demonstrations against the *colons* and Army resistance in Algeria and in France in support of the FLN and Algerian freedom, witnessing the smashed faces of those who had born the brunt of the CRS batons at the front of the demonstration. Maybe he hit Paris at a time of stasis, De Gaulle having resolved the Algerian crisis, the *evénements* of 1968 still to come. Even so, surely he would have been moved by the passionate prose of Franz Fanon, a prose steeped in the poetry of Aimé Césaire. And, just as oddly, there is no hint here of the protest in America against the war in Vietnam. Maybe this is a poetry always seeking transcendence, less concerned with the this-worldly, though in one poem there is a reference to the African, and in what I see as one of Reichert's best poems in the collection *Confessions*(3) there is a remarkably powerful protest poem, Dreaded City: War in the Streets of Baghdad, against the Iraq war, proof that in poetry he can engage with the political.

Reichert is a polymath, poet, painter, novelist, photographer, and there has to be a debate as to whether the same aesthetic can apply to all these various art forms. If spontaneity is all, can this equally apply to poetry as to painting and photography? The very character of being a wordsmith seems to insist on a greater artifice. Expressing language is so inherently artificial. Yet the juvenilia raised for Reichert the aspiration for an absolute honesty of self-expression. And here I think he faced the same challenge as he faces in his painting, `In essence, painting is a manifestation of one's belief in the paradox of true expression.'(*Art & Ego* p79) So there was a challenge of how to get round the influence of his early reading and be absolutely true to this early experience. He has a somewhat odd way of describing the mode of communication. Maybe his is not a need for a direct one-to-one communication. He concludes *Art & Ego*, `We are programmed to live and express ourselves selfishly.' But he continues: `It's only when we bring the mirror up close that nearly everyone sees the same thing.'(p105)

Notes:

1 *Art & Ego: Marcus Reichert in Conversation with Edward Rozzo*, Ziggurat Books, London, 2007

2 Anne V. Zabriskie 1948-1967

3 *Confessions: Poems by Marcus Reichert*, Ziggurat Books International, London & Paris, 2010

I.

Lost Lake

*Eternity is no place for anticipation —
come with me through the maze of forgetting
to the lost lake, where in seclusion we shall,
between the murmurs of my pale violence,
search for the creature of eternal dying.*

1.

Paths in dusk wander past clinging vines,
the pond lies languid below a maze of honeysuckle.
The sylvan gash sleeps where darkness prevails
and rushes heave limpidly with moisture true.

There is a face!
Who are you
wooden woman,
lady of branches?

Frigid rain begins running
as wet as spider's legs,
colder than the icicles
of your whispers:
curving beyond the sphere
of your planet are fluids
dwelling in confusion.

2.

The edges of the iris are taut,
the delicate flesh staring,
its fibrin alert like wire.
Someone is following me
across this sober landscape —
the Rosicrucian believes the rain
comes dripping from his shadow.
But only silence is threatening
this unhindered waste of time,
here in nerve hollow.

3.

In repose, choking boredom gains,
proceeding with anxiety through
the slow fields of visions with
enough power to cause attacks
of confusion, and fear governs
the every move with unknowing.
Regions are entered where insanity
reigns — pools of rainwater to be
spat in as the drapes are pulled.

4.

Moments bright and dull,
yes, like sun and moon,
the door always unlocked
so that both may come
and go, their pilgrimage
winding its way with
the baffling plasticity of duplicity.

An infinite number of identical things
become one: masses of these things
in ovaled sections going in and out
of every orifice, now trapped in me
with no realisation of their existence.
In my revulsion, I fight a mania
very like being crushed to death.

About the guillotine, mock hatred,
mock horror, and then relief
rising in a tumult of applause.

5.

Fantasies of an awakening country
are beyond this imprisoned vision.
These empty chambers are our children,
the moments pretended now vanished,
burnt by a severed sea of promises.

The doors drift closed ending each room —
allow my memory a photograph of
the warm sheets,
the airy blue,
the lank shadow.

Now bend the ray and
carry the light in defiance!

6.

Space is vacant and volume airtight,
the moment forbids all movement.
Silence cowers in the corner as
my breathing shakes the entire world.

Ribs lightly dusted,
a relentless mask,
flesh of the throat,
the smothering latitudes and longitudes,
untamed lethal digressions,
decapitated visions without prey —
now return to the heavenly village,
to the heavy-lidded lake of preoccupation,
as the execution of grey comes and goes.

7.

Closet night in all four corners,
through the gauze of epithelial confinement
shines an Eden of vermilion desecration.
Frail children leap naked about me,
their eyes possessing no life —
the acid scent of feinting flesh.

8.

The fluttering oars now sob
upon the shore — can it be
finished?

Nonchalance enlivens
the telling,
the drugged lunacy
a façade
for the suckling truth.

9.

Eternity calls to an end,
in moments of interruption,
the pollinated sunlight,
paradise of the in-between,
bandage of illusion.

I am waiting for my thoughts
to pounce beyond the earth,
to a place where moss
no longer dwells in the bowels.

March 1963 — December 1967

II.

In the Land of Dirt Farms

In the Land of Dirt Farms: First Half of Childhood

"Forest, I fear you! In my ruined heart your roaring wakens the same agony as in cathedrals when the organ moans and from the depths I hear that I am damned." — Charles Baudelaire

As I prepare to recount these childhood occurrences I remember that there was a deceptive sense of aloneness. Baudelaire teaches us that fear is not the product of isolation but a disobedience to act as (nature's) mediums.* The guilt of prostituting one's own sacred past is a malaise inherent in the deceit of retrospective bargaining perpetrated upon us by our dubiously evolving intellect. We know the affect of this paradoxical deterioration when we can no longer find the thread of our visions, when they are no longer immediate; this betrayal is the antithesis of awakening and results in a polarization of the soul. It is the Judas principal responsible for the loss of our natural gifts as shamans, artists of magic and not contrivance: it is a sorry, atrophying state that must constantly be purged. An excruciating sense of loss is the eventuality of a refusal to act upon our intuition, our weapon against the tedious *abstraction of time*. Life can be an interminable bore and a preposterous hoax without such rites and incantations. We must procure the means to perceive the unknown territories — the interior landscapes — no matter how perplexing or implacable the effort. Only in so doing shall we divine the euphoric fountainhead.

I imagined the sea rising up from its haunches, out of its bays and into the streets, making of them canals that glisten with the stars at night. In summer we travelled across the planes of clover, and then horizons of scrub pine, to the ocean. There it was that the sky loosed its shower of bright images upon me and I found, mouthing their being into language, a melody, erotic and spiritual, to sing. It was essential to escape the sweating walls of our house — those walls pressed inward

and the ceiling came down like a great face made of bread.
In that house I learned that systems of elocution are a kind
of bondage and, when I was forced by anonymous adults
in equally anonymous buildings to recite and decipher
further inanities, I developed a hesitation, a stuttering that
lead me deeper into the privacy of my own language. This
was a language of visions, untethered images that sought an
equation with nature, not with malapropic concepts that had to
be repeated endlessly to be understood.

*So there was the land, and the sea, earth that rolled to the clouds
and lolled in cool hollows, and water that curved deep into its own
supernatural space.*

There were miraculous discoveries. I explored alone, the
elements an automatic Braille, a fearlessness to my wanderings.
I was witness to the roaming water of light. I followed its
imprint in the rouge, the red clay. I saw how the complexion
of the soil is swiftly veined with its coming. There were coarse
thick vines to be emancipated, torn by small hands from
entangled moorings. These served as cords, as springs to carry
or catapult us across the streambed besieged with foul-smelling
sewage, shards of pale emerald glass, and pieces of metal
displaying themselves like rigor-mortised snakes. I often saw
myself drowning in a lost lake of venomous pit vipers and
submerged derelict cars, infinity eclipsing itself in their
surfaces.

A discourse existed in the dirt, in the hard dry-packed stuff
that met my whooping feet, or the mush of mud that could
define the belly from nipples to penis. I inscribed messages
in this tableau, inexplicable codes, signs that delineated
unavailable primitive philosophies, figures that were intuitive
symbols for feelings: the strange sensation of withholding one's
shit from corresponding terrain, or the plea that issues forth in
the fluid of a snapped stem. Spontaneous in its refinement

and verbosely abstruse, it was a fugitive text, aborigine, for no one in particular. It was within this enlightened retreat that the truth of my experience was most eloquently spoken, primordial topographies encountered and described. This atavistic endgame of communication required no scholarly translator, needed no lubricating solution — it produced no regrets because it had no portentous outlet. Later it would be drawn into the enamelled arena of history and death, whirlpool of lime and gibberish, unleashing the infernal pursuing demons of artistic endeavour constantly on a rampage to devour the muse, to digest and defecate her sublime substance.

Silhouetted against the cobalt sky the trees were odd black totems whose aura instilled in me an awe of the dangerous plasticity of my vertical disposition. By nature, we look up to the sun for our light, the stars for our guidance, and we gaze down into the pool at our reflection. Our countenance is imbued with an acute sense of depth, and this permanent aspect startles and enfolds us. Within this realization, this realm of deities revolving and positioning themselves in space, I commenced to act out my own passion play, to proceed as yet unaware of the (mankind's) throne of blood.

In planar format the sprouting exuberance of my psyche twisted and turned, and dashed about feeling the sight of itself in its shadow against the hot naked earth and crossing the board-grey of worn trunks. My dialogue with these certain essences chattered and bounced about the remote eroded quarry abandoned as unfit for the civilizing rake. Sometimes it would reach a screeching intensity, my temples pounding, face gorged to *sanguin*. Then a tumult of thunder and rain hurtling down, leading to a higher plateau of frenzied gesticulation. Peculiar sounds would issue from my throat as if I were metamorphosizing a previously unknown creature. I saw myself away from the fractious local dialect in a clearing protected on its perimeter by this incomprehensible activity.

Without premeditation there was only a constant desire to be there and a longing to be apart — to depart — when in the confines of those who laid claim to my heritage. The intrepid idea of this ritualistic theatre was radiantly incarnate, totally visible to me, however it disappeared as it occurred into the limitless receiving sphere (about me). Obviously it was not conceived to appease the monotonous scanning lens of any viewpoint.

So there was the land, and the sea, earth that rolled to the clouds and lolled in cool hollows, and water that curved deep into its own supernatural space.

Quite early one green morning in July I pushed a beached raft out beyond the breakers, where the waves soothed the soul with a compliant rhythm. We floated, silent, and then, in fits of ecstasy, proclaimed the majesty of the sea and our accomplishment. After some time the sun became too hot, too close, and soaked into our skins, insinuating unspoken distress. Sails of black fins cut the comingling film of the ocean's eye — it was suddenly ponderous in the mystery of its submerged cargo. We didn't cry aloud for fear of encouraging their vigil to action. Finally, after hours of questioning our shrunken destiny, the bronze warriors (life-guards) with their huge shoulders like the heads of gigantic bald eagles made their way to us in a boat the colour of milk. Breathing their cadence, they rowed as pilgrims to an enchanting shore. Safe within that embrace of warm sand, I was aware that my arms were painfully stretched and my palms embrasered from gripping the big rope, our life-line. My thoughts were bleached whiter than muslin, apparitions steamed from the sun's centre, wafted forward and evaporated. The moon was outcast, falling through a hole in my forehead, ordained to be the Pope of the Nether Worlds.

Summer 1965

III.

Poems Written on Glass

1.

the sound of the sea
a shadow moving
unprotected across
the sand

when the shadow walks
into the sunlight
it will no longer be
a mystery of darkness
but a vanishing star

I press its momentary light
to my heart

2.

I said to myself:
the grass is the deepest of greens
the sky is truly immeasurable

life breathes a sweetness into my mouth
emerald waters caress me
and slow low murmurs touch me

3.

self-love
the warmth of one
the moon's pale eye

hot breath in my face
hot limbs about me
burn away
the moon's pale eye

4.

cold rain running
in an open wound
heats my shattered arm
my untouchable arm

the walls climb higher
the anguished pleas
go unacknowledged

slit false hope's despair
pitted guts spilled
chewing the light that dies
blushing breast rises near
beating to bewilder me

5.

the trees warn me
not to return
but only when
I'm here again
will I realize
what I've lost

6.

these memories of you
shall pass as the bird
that sweeps the morning sky

what sullen brutal purpose
to this punishment?

7.

a bird soars
lost in light
gardenia haunting
the breeze

to suffer this sight
without biting thorns
to become a blackbird
fluttering to tear
its pulse apart
its pulse apart

8.

I gazed back through
the mended window
its gleaming stained
my eyes

sentimental scrawlings
on its surface
are repugnant
to the soul
of the horizon
which is innocent
of such betrayals

fires everywhere
illuminate
my shivering
my shattering

9.

the mood
at some forsaken hour
creeps back over me

spasmodic fistfuls
of salt
fill the cracks that split
the scalp and spine
none left
for the leeches
I've squandered it all

jealousy is
the most painful affection
it courts
indifference and thrives
on contempt

10.

what ghostly charm
betrays this lack
of spontaneity
let these frigid days
be gone and never
burn my tongue again

the lazy length
of her body
stretches the rhythm
from corner to corner

11.

amant inconnu

the breezes sing
as does the bell
and I behold a face
too lovely for anything
but glances brief
sanguine glances
that go blank
as seeds sown
under winter skies

12.

beyond the flow of the river's rise
among the thrusting fronds she lies
her thighs beckoning to be caressed
the delirium of her alluring breasts
petulant half-parted lips her fevered
breathing sears the pulsing air as
pinkish petal — delightful pellicle
of the flower — entrances and
possesses with an innocent power
bestowing her selfish gifts amidst
the grass and my pastoral pleas

13.

don't fall back
on my shadow
let your voice
pass over

my temperature
has fallen
I am stronger now
so go on

your legs
like warm water
running in whispers
speak to me
from another room
their words
create a shell

what swimming silence
what delirium
what sustained prey
shall disintegrate
and become
the gaseous hair I seize

subdue
serenitize
inundate me
with serpentine desires

hecklers find me
standing wary naked
in the forest
now show me

what seclusion turns
your cold fire
to liquid
when my words
escape me

you need
no ears
to hear me

14.

so rises a mystery
too lovely to say
in this world
of endless children

perfect solitude is
ripped by the winds
that tear the treasure
of innocence from reach

however encircling are
blindly kneeling waters
allowing old forms
a new place inside

do not falter for
not everything can be
pressed within these
tender billowing things

aura of rose betrays
brief circumstance
disarming the charred
black embrace

15.

a strand of hair threads the universe
as wasted time runs down the soul
a last eyelash erases dreaming hours
as two voices mingle without knowing
submerge
diverge
emerge convergent

water separates from air
to become one in fire
as faces and words abandon their hearts
and fear drives arms to enfold themselves
any place
is its own
destination

nowhere to go but home
ears throbbing numb with fright
a piece of glass as white as milk
becoming unknown breasts unasking
glands of dust
the everlasting
branch is filled with blood

it drinks in dread
and gives out floating

June 1964 — May 1966

IV.

Diary of the Plague

Dereliction

The city with its schedules of need has become a volcanic fester beneath the sun. I have heard someone's voice and I have been touched by their unknowing hand, two chords have collided. What pain shall I relinquish, or torture embrace in ascendancy? Is stair-step time so easily vaulted? The contorted realms of so-called golden days now seem euphoria. The Prussian green of odd pines, the phantom dervishes that scarfed from hill to trickling valley, are silhouettes against the light with its warm enfolding haze. I have been carried away from pond and fern to watchful towers in the sky. From my balcony I view the terrible beauty of the noonday moon and, in waiting for the night's visitation, I know the silent exquisite moments of eternity.

Varicella swim thickly throughout, no panacea,
no sedation, no blooming aesthetic of Venus,
no veil of serenity, no paradisial ovum and semen.

A balneation of bilge and offal flows through the streets, insalubriousness breeds in unattended-to afflictions, varicella swim thickly throughout. One can hear the gurgling of the sewers besieged with viscous discharge. Lethargic films subdue all thought of antidotal retaliation, obliteration pumps through florid temples. Bereavement etherizes the air between strangers, a multitude of hands trembling in isolation: there are no doctors, there is no army. The trees bend with bodies and razors grieve the wrist, curfewed children perch on dead men's coffins. They are the innocents who, on the precipice of knowledge, feel the metal of their legs turn to mush.

Betrayed by lunatic words I accepted to speak, I see myself beyond the bodies of sight, an alien. My life is vacant, a lugubrious symposium of decay — questioning, never hearing any answers. I lie awake at night and watch the neon sign across the roofs throb to the beat of my heart. Each morning the space increases as I slither from my bed to lie beneath the universe that floats in the tub. Sitting and watching the silent dust filter through the blinds, the faces below itching with mosquito bites, I notice that the curtains are paler. The room is a forest of torn wallpaper. The aroma of objectivity mingles with the summer honeysuckle and, as I do every night, I watch two people dancing on their veranda. Their laughter, a rendezvous of shattered vases, is like rain that daresn't wash away the darkness.

*Obliteration pumps through your flowering temples
as they incinerate the infested in a garden in Sochi.*

Delirium

A discordant tone scythes at my eardrums. I feel the atom gone berserk, it is a rodent, crazy and bloated in starving, that rips and claws at the walls of the cell. Up against its furious talons, the molecule's puckered, pouting, complacent membrane gives way and the entire network of seething, restless channels is opened and reeling in aberration. Simultaneously a shot rips across the nerves of Versailles, the mirrored halls of synapse. Recognition of total physical upheaval comes in drooling waves of shock, slowly, from beneath layer upon layer of mutilating tissue. It is a kind of eerie suffocation, verbose in its gaps, and stifling in the stillness and awesome plasticity of its strangulation. Life has become a laborious judgement, without reply. There is a cancer in the soul.

Curving beyond the sphere of the planet are fluids dwelling in confusion. Seminal sojourn, floating on a river of no return, day-long breezes murmur until shadows on the water become orange thoughts that flood the horizon — perpetual foaming dawn. Infants in unison, their green teats peeking, look out to sea. They sing of the prefect ballet leg and peninsular campaigns. Continents of the Great Mind have abandoned them, giving up their symbolic parenthood to the inundation. My hands are etched with their wetness, I have committed innominate incest upon them...I, the benevolent keeper of my atrophied erection, have, with the same erection, fucked the abyss...

And what of my mother and father, who most certainly are dead? Statues of black mud who carried stories of the burning crosses, of the superstitious and their losses, out of the coal regions. They'd lived on the edge of a misshapen cliff. Now their voices — in vacant rooms — come shimmering across the roofs with recitations of the past, a morbid entrancing past. The steadfast dialect of their eyes punctures my untruths. Mine is an intricate scar.

But I have also committed crimes against myself, in-between ruined maps of no heartbeat, in dim lit hallways. Idolater of my own sex, the hair between my legs was Braille. Kidnapped within territories of self, no one knew. Determined as a long distance swimmer, my penis stole onward with no thought of ordeal. Masturbating into a rose-scented glove, I was ordered off the immaculate sofa like a dog with no claws, having a vague memory of guts sliding towards the drain of a butcher house floor. My mongrel semen meandered down dusty trestles. I was the atrocious pariah who had slunk into the house to murder the ordained. Tremors of revulsion had twitched at the corners of my eyes. I had wanted the faultless windows of their houses smeared shut with my excrement.

Imagine tuxedo suits, cloth of the high priests, in flames in the forest, hung up in the trees.

You must triumph over this mental clamour,
your sublime elevator winging dimly through
the living-room day — bagnio oh, oh, oh —
song of the epidermis, endearment of scotophilia,
temperature 98.6, divine pellicle be inundated
with desire, the sun's ray a light-year of innocence.
Now tell me — will your vehicle find its way to
the promised land lacking deciphered words?

Deluge

To the sailor, as yet in pubescence, the world is a mummified fish, a ghastly calm in its eye: my hook is lodged in that gorge of sallow pink linoleum gums. Now I'm hallucinating a refuge, a woman beckoning from a grey-gunnelled boat that circles the Towers of Neuron, spectral threads left in its wake going black before gold to become human hair. Can you hear me, so far away? Oh, these flooded boulevards with their willowy aspects.

I swim through the sphacelation to find her collapsed at the bottom of the boat with the maggots. And, after what seems innumerable days of cresting the warm mucilage, I secretly feel her vulva under which no vagina exists and brush my fingers across her chest where there are no nipples, and I withdraw my hand with a start for the pin that fastens her garment has gone into my palm. Scarlet bubbles purple in the blue light. I watch with fascination as she feeds on me...vampire gestation period, catalyst of circulatory cities, language of oxygen, and verb of blood.

Or am I, alone in this trance, the beaten nigger in the boat, his blooming arrogance marooned on a compost of wooden boards, looking into the mire at his mocking, fallow reflection? The planes of his face are missing, his skull shows through, and his eyes are holes from which great dragonflies and snails escape.

Having shed my skin, the basin of the hull, full of piss and sedimentary carbons, is my soothing, fatal bath. And the woman beside me, who moans her sinus dirge to the rattle of the oar-locks, becomes in turn each female figure of love and authority I had hoped to forget. She is a corpse but steadily grows larger, until the fabric of her dress is a splendorous bat-wing sail that looms to black out the cloying sky. Split-second landscapes vanish about me, my pigment slipstreams over the edge and light, transversing stars, transports my image to no surface, my form transfixed.

1962 — 1972

V.

Darkness: Selected Poems

Blood Flower

The aimless tracings of half-hearted lips
carouse these unspoken boundaries.
Mocking lips, transparencies of impurity,
mimic me as you tell uncertain truths,
your umbra rising moonward,
obese with the promise of deliverance.

I took from your mouth
a vision of you dead,
it burned the tongue
of passion in my head.

October 1964

Day of Africa

Daylight postponing darkness,
not the other way around, slow
extermination of balmy evening,
the crickets making their sound.

Our mouths wide open waiting,
a winged man emerges and soars.
He sees the green rush disturbed
and hastens with the sighs of night,
then hovers over the ethereal pillar,
black wings blown about his figure.

Today is the day of Africa, he calls.

Now he descends,
recalling the naked faces
in their dreaming,
and slips between
the thin sliver of blink,
into the twin ditches
of death and sleep.

Spring 1965 — Paris

Destroying the Vestiges

Destroying the vestiges,
the forlorn remnants
of unpleasant hope,
becomes an act of mercy.

Finally giving up the guilt
of prostituting one's
own sacred past
is in the process of
the polarization of the soul —
revolving in
pure blank countenance
about the ether,
waiting for a likely vessel
to pour into.

All deciphered occurrences
do not constitute acts,
especially when confused
with symbols fingered in mud.

March 1972

The Shaman Leaps

The shaman leaps to erase the barrier reefs,
he speaks without moving his mouth:
never go this way once hoping to return...

He is a walking corpse
with fathomless eyes
knowing mysterious regions
where radiation is worshipped.

He speaks the purple embrace of death,
his tales, fartherest from the tongue,
steal awareness from the earth —
there is no time to read a sign
as stray dogs follow our scent.

Unlikelihood's birthday of severed umbilical,
lines of undoing melting into lines of remembrance,
the tree did bend with my body,
the razor grieved my wrist,
the curfewed child sat on the dead father's coffin,
as once again I did hold the breath within
and images within their nonsense returned
freed from the placidly curving turret.

Oh the lovely wall
of glass bone,
Oh the lamentable wall of Endymion
and Lamina Propria,
Oh the insidious high-pitched wall
of neuron,
Oh the wall,
Oh the monolith!

1963 — 1964

The Sabine Women

I saw the Sabine women,
their grasping fists,
their crushing pinions,
their rouged buttocks flinching —
I placed the gleaming blade on the step.

I observed the maidens bathing
beyond the tree trunks,
massive steeds raging
with slimy monsters
between their hooves.

Seamen adoring the triumphant Amphitrite,
I wear a long white gown to cover my solidity,
a cigarette burning in the vacuum of the tunnel.

August — October 1963

The Angel Morpheus

White scobe opens a window
at the sinister cocktail party
and the last dream
beyond Outer Mongolia,
as well as the bright sleep
of all-consuming reverie,
glow like the Angel Morpheus.

Medicinal mediums resurrected
with shining syringes are nothing
if not the alien dust
in the alabaster ashtray
as blots of black ink make
a spattered sketch of cirrus clouds.

Peering into the examination box
where the beautiful girls
put on their false eyelashes,
I'm aware of the vast horizons
of my once barren intestines
now digesting lotus pools of light.

Soft flesh in its white cups,
and her voice,
slip into an envelope manifest
quite unexpectedly
by the catastrophe of upholstery
and rubbery comedy about me —
glycerine fills my glass.

But I am invisible among
the withered daughters of winter,
diaphanous blue effervescing

with languid resign upon
the tangled hair of the rouged man.

My eyes are freezing,
I'm a void of flesh —
I've been hypnotized
by your complacent
face...so smooth, so
full of nothing. I want
a solitary prison,
a plump heart
before the kill.

Spring 1965 — Paris

Young Pagan Journeying

Young pagan journeying through me,
fear circling about the cushions of my
helplessness, the physics of love have
dissipated. The flying dagger presses
closer and blue danger gathers up
the earth in its teeth. Nerves throb
and fold into electric vessels now
illuminating the angels who protect
children. Lifted to the lilt of chimes
upon the towering face, darkness
threatens the frail frightened streets.
Can you hear me, so far away…far
from these streets with their willowy
aspects? As the sun seeks fire, we
seek the sequence unended. But
the overpowering sky presses down
as luminous caverns and vaporous
passages wash away in torrents
of steep shadows. Chewing the scars
in a greasy whisper, all have lifted
silver sleeves, and dripping resounds
inside everyman's skull. The air
exists as blue burns the retina and
infinity beckons all shadows to
become one as a grey-bottomed boat
crests the trees, golden threads left
in its wake fragrant as human hair.

October 1967 — Providence

Hymn of the Sacred Heart

The vile spring upon the hill
rises with Lucifer in the morning
and there is fire everywhere.
Your inventor's compassionate penis
wriggles in his hand like a lamprey,
ready to dart in and out of
the bursting virgins' bulrushes.
His sanctuary is littered with
the mangled meat of last night's
sepulchre and his temple echoes
with the shrill patterns carved
in the tenderloin, the unveiling
tattooed on his sullen eyelids,
but we are subdued as blood drips
from Christ's plastered rib and
once more these thorned hearts
of ours are soaked in holy light.
The needle slides in with graceful
black fingers and the eighth realm
is death destroyed, the realm
in which nails have failed —
plastic tents postponing the cold,
flesh pressed rigid to glass cages,
narcotic saints in petrified pieces.

The hymn of the sacred heart plays
in the heat as we mouth the rosary
thorns and the wedding massacre begins.

August 1965

Man Swimming

There was a man
swimming in a river,
the water too deep
for him to wade.
He swam neither to
the left nor the right,
neither did he rest for
this was the icy water
that had frozen within
her face and slipped
so very silently from
her mouth in the spring.

October 1964

As Mortals Build Edifices

As mortals build edifices of immortal dreams,
the thoughts come spilling and the ink bleeds out,
the lapse in my innards drifting upon Aegean waters.
Voluptuous impulses rippling, a salvatory page lands
in the state of the somnolent atman, the idiot carrying
his water in thimblefuls down the road to the hole.

Past fountains of glass, her victims transparent,
the fictional Aphrodisia enlivens my weak flesh
as I sink in her ooze, her apprentices helotic,
starkly satanic, ghastly, their hands lingering
about my translucent loins, and I naturally ask:
will she resist in a fit of epileptic whimpering?

Nerve centres on consequence courses drive
their teeming scorpions through our embrace.
Timid man with his cleaver loathes the pouches
swollen with hot corpuscles, and so he stalks
the adoring cocks, deaf-mute residing in his eyes,
invalid gesturing, as if ably departing the menace.

Lick the red brides
and send them thirsting
into the weeds.

March 1963

Roses of Remanence

I'm going to
cut roses
of *remanence*
soon after
your death,
that they
may accompany
you into
the ground.

I'll have
their throats
cut quickly,
pick the thorns
from their limbs.

I'll light one
and place it
burning inside
your mouth,
then close
your lips and
lock the earth.

September 1966

Rimbaud Knelt Helplessly

Rimbaud knelt helplessly between
the Abyssinian's dusty legs
as the jewel of Luxor scalded
his tongue beyond supplication.

Artaud died high on a promontory
in the Tarahumara Mountains muttering:
If one stated that non-entity was or is,
that non-entity existed or exists,
then would also state that there is
existence — the existence of nothingness.

December 1967 — Providence